Is Your Business *Google-Able?*

Small Business Local Marketing
Methods Are Changing Fast, Are
Your Marketing Tactics Keeping
Up With The Times?

Is Your Business Listed In Google?
If So, How Many Times?
Can Potential Clients Find You Fast?
Even If They Don't Know You Exist?

A Crash Course in Mobile Local Marketing
by

Charles P. Kassotis

Income Disclaimer

This document contains business strategies, marketing methods and other business advice that, regardless of my own results and experience, may not produce the same results (or any results) for you. I make absolutely no guarantee, expressed or implied, that by following the advice below you will make any money or improve current profits, as there are several factors and variables that come into play regarding any given business.

Primarily, results will depend on the nature of the product or business model, the conditions of the marketplace, the experience of the individual, and situations and elements that are beyond your control.

As with any business endeavor, you assume all risk related to investment and money based on your own discretion and at your own potential expense.

Is Your Business
Google-Able?

Small Business Local Marketing
Methods Are Changing Fast, Are
Your Marketing Tactics Keeping
Up With The Times?

Is Your Business Listed In Google?
If So, How Many Times?
Can Potential Clients Find You Fast?
Even If They Don't Know You Exist?

A Crash Course in Mobile Local Marketing
by

Charles P. Kassotis

TABLE OF CONTENTS

Introduction 9

Are You Leaving Money on the Table? 11

Center of Influence Marketing 27

How to Find Customers for Life 35

The Referral Marketing Goldmine 45

How to Tear Down Customer Resistance 61

The *Right* Way to Place Yellow Page Ads 75

Getting Online - Where To Start 85

What About Facebook - Is It Worth My Time? . 93

Analytics Are The Key To Your Success 117

5 Proven Internet Strategies to Explode Your
Local Sales 131

About the Author 135

Introduction

Do you know what the most profitable skill is for running a small business?

It's not keeping the shelves stocked. It's not managing employees. It's not even having a good product.

No. The most important skill is *marketing your business*. Why? Well, the only time you can bring money into your business is if you *sell* something. You can't stock the shelves unless you have money to buy the stuff to put on the shelves.

And you can't pay your employees unless you have money come in the business from selling stuff. A good product might as well be a piece of junk in a box if nobody knows it exists.

That's where marketing comes in. It's how you communicate to the public that you have a good product, that you offer a good consumer experience and that they should buy stuff from you, rather than one of your competitors.

Marketing is also the most misunderstood skill on the planet. Poor Marketing is perhaps why

65% of new businesses close their doors after 2 years, and over 85% of businesses don't make it 8 years before going under.

Most of your competition simply does not understand how to do marketing properly to bring in amazing results, in little to no time. So just knowing a few simple things will put you at a great advantage.

In the land of the blind, the person with one eye is KING!

You are about to learn the 7 most powerful – and profitable – marketing strategies that you can start using today to become the "king" in your own local marketplace within 3 months time.

The last three chapters will take those strategies to a whole new level, expanding your reach exponentially by exploding your online presence.

You have right now, in your hands, information that could change your life forever. Use it and profit from it.

All the best,

Charles P. Kassotis

Are You Leaving Money on the Table?

Do you know the 3 Deadly Mistakes that almost all small businesses are making? If you don't, you are not alone. Most entrepreneurs simply have never considered the fact that by making these 3 small tweaks to their current business, they can increase sales by up to 40% within the next 60 days. It's absolutely true.

I know that some of these ideas will shock you... And in fact I hope they do. Why? Because my job is to help you take a fresh look at your own business, and evaluate the areas that can be improved *right now* in order to create more sales & improve your bottom line immediately.

MISTAKE #1: GOING AFTER NEW CUSTOMERS

Yes, you read that right. New customers are the most expensive people in the world to find, attract into your place of business, and then convert into customers.

To help you understand this, let me demonstrate to you a powerful fact.

There are only 3 ways to increase your profits.

The first way is to increase your number of customers. If you have a lemonade stand and sell 100 cups a day to 100 people and make $0.10 a cup, you make a total of $10 a day in profit... If you figure out a way to get 200 people to buy a cup, you've just doubled your profits.

But that's not the only way you can double your profit. What if you figure out a way for your customers to purchase two cups of lemonade each? By doing so, you will be able to double your profits with the same number of customers.

And what if you were to offer something for your customers to purchase that is complimentary to the lemonade... such as a hot dog? Then, if a certain percentage *also* buys a hot dog when you sell them lemonade, you can increase your sales even more.

So let's review: short of cutting expenses, cutting corners and raising the prices, which by the way, is never enough in the long run, here are the only three ways that you will ever be able to to grow your businesss and increase your profits:

1. Get More Customers

2. Sell More Stuff to the Same Customers

3. Same customers making more frequent purchases

Of the three, which is the most profitable? Well, let's look at it like this. Let's say you spend $2,500 a year on a yellow page ad, and it brings you in 100 prospective customers.

You have paid $25 for each person that has come into your store who *might* purchase from you. That is a static cost. You pay that $25 if they buy nothing from you, or if they buy everything in the store.

So what if you could increase the average transaction value of each customer by just $10? What would it cost you? Usually, nothing but a few minutes of creative thought. You've already paid $25 to get them in the store so you might as well maximize their value.

In the case of the lemonade stand, you "cross-sold" them on a hot dog. It's just a matter of creatively packaging complimentary goods and using the right language to get the highest number of people to say yes to buying something in addition to what they originally came in to the store to purchase.

McDonald's simply asks: "Do you want fries with that?" Extra cost for McDonald's to do that: 2 seconds of training for the employee, and 2 seconds for the employee to say it to each customer.

The result: an overall bump of about $0.08 in profit *per customer*. And when you have "over 1 billion served", that's a lot of profit!

So here's rule number 1: Spend more of your advertising budget and time on figuring out how to get customers who have purchased from you in the past, or your new prospects, to PURCHASE MORE from you.

Often times the last thing you need is more customers. Whatever problems you currently have in your business usually multiplies when you bring more customers into the funnel. Instead, figure out how to get MORE from the same number of customers.

Which brings us to Rule Number 2: You must figure out how to get your existing customers to make more frequent purchases from you!

Here's everything required in order to make your marketing work.

- They have to KNOW you exist

- They have to want and be able to afford what you offer

- They have to trust you

You see, new customers first need to hear about you. But that's not enough. They also have to be in the market for what you offer. It's hard to sell ice cream to Eskimos.

And finally, they have to trust you enough to exchange their hard-earned dollars for the value you promise to deliver to them.

Your current customers, on the other hand, already know you exist, and have already demonstrated that they need at least some of what you offer, and at least at one point in their life they trusted you enough to exchange their dollars for the value you promised them.

All else being equal, who do you think is going to be more inclined to say yes to your next offer? A stranger -- or someone who knows you and is likely to be comfortable dealing with you again?

I think the answer is obvious. Before we go into how to get past customers to increase the frequency from which they purchase from you, let's first deal with increasing the average purchasing size from each customer.

MISTAKE #2: NOT EFFECTIVELY USING CROSS-SELLS, UP-SELLS OR "PACKAGE" SELLING

We already discussed "cross sells" with the "do you want fries with that?" example. So what does this mean for your business? The first thing you need to do is implement your own cross-sells.

Here's a simple way to do that. Look at your 5 to 7 most popular sellers in your business. Each one of them should have a cross-sell. For example in the flooring business, when people buy carpeting, you should also have a special offer for them to buy "spot remover" along with their carpeting.

You can even give them a special "purchase discount" because you don't need as high a margin since you have already PAID (in marketing and advertising) to attract them to come in the door and purchase from you.

So select your five biggest sellers, and find other items that you can offer that complement these main purchases, just like fries compliment a cheeseburger.

17

Then, just create a quick script to use and to train your employees to use this technique. It could be something as simple as "Would you be interested in receiving a special 60% purchaser discount on spot remover to complement your flooring purchase today?"

Anything is better than nothing. Based on tests, even a weak attempt at a cross-sell works 6%-20% of the time. The point being is that cross sells have almost no hard cost at all to implement, so why not do it?

The second thing is the up-sell. This is where you try to offer them a more premium version of what they are ready to purchase. Let's return to the flooring example.

There are different pads you can put under your carpet. There is the basic pad, often made of several different materials that are bonded together, thus making it cheaper to sell to the client. Then there is "prime" pad, which is solid, more durable, makes the flooring last longer, but is more expensive.

In this case, when putting together an offer for the customer, you'd want to say something like "Would you like to invest a little bit more to make this carpet last 6 years longer – and feel more comfortable under your feet?"

Then, you simply explain why buying the upgraded version of the padding is a better option for them.

Now think about it – if your markup is the same for both types of padding, then you'll make more money if you sell them the more expensive carpet pad. Example: let's say you make 50% profit on each pad you sell. If a customer needs 100 square yards of the basic pad, and that sells for $4.50 per square yard, then you just sold $450 of materials, of which $225 is profit to you.

But what if you could've bumped them up to the premium pad that sells for $7.50 per square yard? Now that's $750 in material sold, of which $375 is profit to you.

That's an increase of $150 for just a *few minutes* of sales work. Again, all you have to do is come up with a simple script, and a simple way to demonstrate why the little bit of extra cost involved for the customer is worth the investment in terms of what they're going to get for that little extra bit of cost.

So how can you make this work for you? Go back to those 5-7 popular products and simply ask yourself -- "Is there an upgraded and/or premium version of this that I can offer to my customers?"

There always is. And often times, you can *make* a premium version without hardly any additional hard cost, if you focus on *intangibles*. Let me give you an example.

Let's say you own a high-end restaurant. One premium version you can offer to your clients is the "immediate seating" club. For a small fee each year, these customers can guarantee that they get seated as soon as they enter the restaurant.

In this case, you're selling time and convenience, not a product. That has a lot of value in this day and age.

Or you could even create a special area for preferred customers that has a much more luxurious feel to it, to make them enjoy the atmosphere more. Again, you're selling luxury, not a product... another intangible.

The final sales technique you should consider using is "Packaged Selling". Most people prefer to have someone else make the decision for them, so they don't have any responsibility in the matter.

Let's return to the flooring example. Why not create an "Active Lifestyle Package". This would be for people with young children, maybe pets as well, or for those who have high traffic homes.

For this special package, you choose the carpet, padding, vinyl and tile options, and then sell it as a package, instead of each component on its own. This allows you to already INCLUDE the premium versions, or the products that have the highest profit margins.

Your customers are more likely to say yes, if you do it right, since it's easier for them to say yes.

Then, the next logical step is to up-sell them to an even more deluxe package. Why not?! In this case it could be the "Active but Luxurious Lifestyle Package."

Let's go back to our restaurant example. Let's design the "Romance Package". In this case, the customer would get a limo to pick them up at their door, they get a special table near the fireplace that is more secluded, they get a vase filled with beautiful flowers that they get to take home and keep (including the vase), and they get a special "Lover's Dessert" for the lucky couple to share.

You're no longer in the restaurant business... you're in the romance business... and you can charge a lot more for that!

At the very least, you need to create one "package" that you can offer to a certain portion of your clients. Make it much higher priced and more luxurious than normal so that even if only a handful of customers say yes to it each year, you'll have made a pretty good extra bit of profits without doing hardly any more work.

MISTAKE #3: NOT UNDERSTANDING THE LIFETIME VALUE OF A CUSTOMER

If you knew the potential lifetime value of even an average customer, you'd spend far more time making sure existing customers continued to use your services, and far less time trying to get new customers.

Let me give you an example. Let's say Lucy is 45 and spends $100 a week at her preferred grocery store. Lucy doesn't plan on moving any time soon, and has at least 15 more years of good shopping left in her.

So let's see, 15 years is 780 weeks. And at an average of $100 a week, that's $78,000. If you owned that grocery store, don't you think it would be prudent to come up with a strategy to make sure Lucy keeps coming back to you?

Now get this. A famous study done 20 years ago, that was recently just re-tested and re-confirmed, found out what causes people to quit going to a store or a service provider. Here are the results.

9% - Leave because of competition

OK, so someone else might come along offering them a better deal, or better service. Or perhaps they have a location that's closer than yours. It sucks, but that is part of the game. And it doesn't mean that you can't get them back with a little creativity, but again, it's only 9%.

9% - Leave because they move

It's hard to get someone to come back to your store if they move halfway across the country. It's just the nature of the beast. Some will move because we are by nature nomadic creatures. Do you offer a shipping program?

14% - Leave because of a complaint or dissatisfaction with the service or product.

Okay, this can be worked on a bit, but one thing I've learned in business is that you can't please everyone all the time, nor do you want to. Anyway, it's not that big of a deal, because there is something FAR, FAR greater that causes your customers to go somewhere else.

It is greater than all these other factors combined. Here it is:

68% - Leave because of perceived apathy of the service provider.

In other words, they feel you only look at them as a customer to get money from, and that you don't care about them. Notice the word *perceived*. You might very well care about them, but if you don't show them you care about them in a way that's unique and that isn't something that everyone else does, then there is no reason for them to remain loyal to you.

So if you don't have a specific "customer retention" strategy in place, you're losing 2/3rds of your previous customers! When you consider the potential lifetime value of a customer, that should make you sick to your stomach!

So what's the remedy? First, you need to increase the amount of communication you have with your past customers. At the very least, follow the "4 a day rule". Every business day, someone in your business should contact at least 4 past customers with a personal follow up, either by email, phone, letter or in person.

You should also consider a newsletter... and no, not those fancy, beautiful and "corporate looking" newsletters I'm sure your familiar with. You need to take a more personal approach.

People don't fall in love with corporations. They fall in love with personalities. The first part of that word is "person". You have to open up to them. Let them know who you are and a little bit about what's going on in your life. You also have to show some character and a bit of humor, and style.

Think of why you're close friends with the friends you're close with. You should try to establish that same bond with your customers. There are several strategies I use to do this, one of them is with a monthly newsletter.

Finally, someone who cares about you looks out for your best interest with no ulterior motive in mind. Again, that's where a newsletter comes in handy. Each month, you can create an article giving them tips on how to better their life, improve the value they can get from your services, and just things that can make them feel better about themselves. And they're getting all this stuff just because they're a customer of yours.

That's how you make someone feel special.

At any rate, you need to create some kind of customer retention campaign, and that's often just staying in contact with past customers, once every few months to let them know you're still thinking about them.

Center of Influence Marketing

Normal advertising is a complete waste of money. Why? Because normal advertising will get you normal results. You don't become an industry leader or a dominant presence by doing things the "normal" way.

Most small businesses advertise in the Yellow Pages. Really, still. However, I think you're going to find Yellow Page advertising is going to be gone the way of the Dodo soon, because more people now use the Internet to find their information than ever before. More on that later.

Besides, almost all Yellow Page ads look the same. Hmmmm... could it be because they're all designed by the same person? Of course, this means that everybody's ad is (by definition) "normal".

Newspaper advertising is also falling. But let's look at it – again almost all the ads look the same. Same generic sizes and placement, they're almost hard to see regardless of how creative the copywriter gets. If everything looks the same, everybody gets the same results. Same is Lame.

Finally, consider this – you're advertising in the same place as your competitors. That's kind of dumb, isn't it? I'd rather advertise in a vacuum, where I'm the only choice.

You have to think outside the box. I fashion myself as a collector of good ideas. I look for those different ways of advertising that don't get normal results... but extraordinary results.

What I'm about to show you is going to give you a far greater return than normal advertising ever will. It will also dramatically enhance the relationship you have with your fellow business owners and finally it'll just make others think you're some sort of genius because of your innovation.

I'm talking about center of influence marketing. Here's the premise – instead of going out hunting down your ideal prospects, what would happen if you already went to where a bunch of them hang out, and just put your sign up in front of them?

You're going to where they already are, instead of picking them up "one by one" in the newspaper, on the television, or in the Yellow Pages.

Okay, so here's what you're going to do – you're going to come up with a bunch of different places where your ideal customers frequent in large numbers. Then you're going to construct an offer that will allow you to siphon those ideal customers off into your own sales funnel. And, it's only going to cost you a small "toll booth" fee to do this, which you will only pay out of a portion of the profits you're generating.

Let' take a second to talk about targeted marketing. Say you and I both owned a pizza place. I would only need one competitive advantage, and I could destroy you and win every single customer. I'd give you all other advantages, because, when totaled, they still wouldn't give you a chance.

Yes, I would give you the best ingredients. I'd give you the best employees. I'd give you the best location. I'd give you the coolest store layout. I'd only ask for one thing...

I'd only ask that all my customers are dying of hunger!

When someone is hungry, they don't care what your store looks like. They don't care if you have good service. They don't care if the food even tastes good. They are just so hungry that they'll practically pay anything and eat anything to satisfy that hunger.

What targeted marketing does is isolates and focuses your efforts on singling out those who are "hungriest" for whatever you offer.

Let me make it real to you. Let's say you're in the retail flooring business. Okay, now people who buy flooring... what else do they tend to need that complements that?

Well, a lot of people who need flooring also need paint. What would happen if you had a majority of the paint stores sending the customers who needed flooring your way?

If I wanted to market to small businesses to offer my marketing consultation services, where would I go? Well, I'd start with the local accountants, because they help a lot of business owners with their taxes.

I would also go to the heads of trade associations that small business owners would be a member of (like the chambers of commerce, for example), and volunteer for free to give a speech where I'd share my expertise on how to get more customers.

I would go to attorneys that help people form corporations, and attorneys who specialize in helping small businesses.

See what I'm doing here? I'm finding a complementary, non-competitive business entity that already attracts the "hungry" customers that I'm in search of. Instead of having to find those customers myself, I'm leveraging their efforts.

Now, here's how to NOT make this work. Go up to one of these centers of influence and say, "Hey, why don't you tell your customers to come to me when they need X." This is completely ridiculous.

You have to make it make sense for them to refer others to you before they will. What's an easy way to do this? Why not say, "Hey, I know from time to time you have customers that also need my services. So how do you feel about this? Every time you send someone over my way, and they become my customer, I give you X% of the sale?"

Warning – in some industries, it's illegal to do this. And since I'm no lawyer, check the laws first to make sure that you can legally do this. I'm just giving you one example here. There are other ways you can reward them.

For example, send customers to *them* in return. It could be as simple as making a stack of fliers up to put in their business, and they do likewise to distribute at your business. Now it's a "referral revolving door" and more importantly... it's a win-win situation.

Here's how you can make it work for you. First, pull out the Yellow Pages. Go through them, and each time you find a category that would be complementary to your business, write it down.

Get 5-10 different complementary "industries", and then pick the top 3 businesses in each of those industries. Now you have a list of 15-30 businesses to approach.

Second, create your irresistible offer for these businesses. If you can give them a cash incentive for a referral, then consider that as your offer. Or come up with something equally enticing that answers their number one question -- "What's in it for me?"

Another thing you can do here is to give a special offer just for *their* customers. It could be a discount, or something extra they get for free that you would normally charge for. This way, the "What's in it for me?" is that their customers will like them more, because it looks like the owner went to bat and negotiated a special deal just for them.

How many businesses could you do this with? Well, as many as you would like. This can take care of the new customer acquisition end of things, especially when you combine it with referral marketing.

Think about it – you could easily get ten businesses that were complementary to you to promote for you for some sort of incentive.

For some, it might just be that you put up some fliers at the counter, with a special "freebie" just for their customers. For other businesses, it might be a customer exchange. You send customers their way if they send customers your way. For others still, it might work to downright pay them a cut of the sales.

In any case, realize the importance behind this – most of the cost for customer acquisition will only be paid after the customer is acquired. You pay a percentage of the sale – after the sale is made. You get referrals because you refer.

This truly takes the risk out of advertising, because you'll only pay for it if it works. Not a bad deal!

How to Find Customers for Life

Imagine that there was a huge amount of oil buried right outside in your backyard. We're talking millions of dollars worth.

Would that make you rich? Not if you didn't know about it! You could live your whole life sitting on "liquid gold" and be none the wiser.

However, if I came up to you and told you about it, and showed you beyond a shadow of doubt that there was oil and you drilled for it. Then you'd be filthy rich.

In most small business, there DOES exist a situation that is similar to the oil well example above. Most small business owners are sitting on a potential fortune and they don't even realize it.

In this chapter I'm going to share with you perhaps the single most effective strategy for mining the "hidden gold" that is likely to exist in your business.

THE FORGOTTEN "RULE" OF AN OBSCURE ITALIAN ECONOMIST

In 1906 a man by the name of Vilfredo Pareto discovered something unusual about the Italian economy – 80% of the wealth was controlled by 20% of the population.

Was this just an anomaly? Turns out it wasn't. In Britain he found the same thing to be true and found it to be true in pretty much all economies. But what's interesting is that this unequal distribution exists outside of economies as well. For example, studies have shown in general that:

80% of traffic accidents are committed by 20% of drivers

80% of crimes are committed by 20% of the population

80% of a company's output comes from 20% of its employees, and most importantly of all...

80% of your profits come from <u>only</u> 20% of your customers!

This is almost always true. So what's that mean for you?

Simple: if you can isolate who those "20 percenters" are, and then come up with a marketing plan that will attract more customers like those "20 percenters" and also create additional products, services and offers for your "20 percenters" then...

You should be able to, very easily, add 20% to your bottomline profits within the next 90 days.

WHERE TO START

In an ideal situation, you've kept track of your past customers purchases, so you can access their records. What you want to do is go through and first isolate customers who have spent the *most* money with you.

Now, that doesn't necessarily mean that they are your most profitable customers. They are just your highest grossing customers. Unfortunately, gross does not always mean more profitable! However, it's a good place to start.

After you find your highest grossing customers, then analyze your profit margin on those customers, to narrow it down even more. To make it easy for you, come up with your 50 "highest grossing customers", and out of those 50, arrange them in order of *most profitable*, in terms of percentages.

Now take your 20 "Most profitable" customers, and analyze them. What we are looking for are demographics and psychographics.

Demographics are things such as:

- Size of Household

- Annual Income Earned

- Age

- Gender

- Geographical Location

Psychographics are:

- What clubs they belong to
- What their hobbies and interests are
- Their Values
- Their Opinions
- Lifestyle & other behavior attributes

In other words, you are trying to isolate their "culture" if you will.

How can this be helpful to you? Well, let's say you analyze your results and find out that your most profitable customers are typically:

White, aged 45-50, have 2-3 children, are married, live on the northeast side of town, make between $75,000 to $100,000 a year, are active in the community, especially with charitable events, typically play a lot of golf and/or tennis, are conservative republicans, and often take 2-3 vacations a year.

That's some valuable information! For starters, did you know you can rent a list in your area with those "selects" (select is just a fancy term for different attributes).

Yes, for a fee you could get a list of all the people in your city that are between 45-50, living in a certain zip code, making an annual income of $75,000 to $100,000 a year. And that's just a few of the "selects" you can specify. You can even go deeper if you wish.

These are the type of prospects you want to spend your money marketing to! While past results do not necessarily guarantee future behavior, they are about as good an indicator to go by as any. The point is, if that type of customer was profitable to you in the past, it stands to reason similar people who fit that description will also be extremely profitable for you NOW.

Then what do you do? The best thing is to create a direct mail campaign and send a letter to each name on the list you rented making them a special offer.

You want to write an advertisement that is personable, explains the benefits of your services, and makes a special "introductory offer" to get them into your place of business.

Even better is if, in those advertisements, you talk about things like golf and tennis, taking vacations, saying things that conservative republicans are known to agree with, and talk about charitable events. This helps build rapport with the prospect. You just have to tie those things to your sales message and offer in some creative way.

And that's just one simple example of how to make the "80/20" rule work in your favor.

Here's an even better example: Look into your customer records of your most profitable customers and ask yourself, "What services and goods can I offer them that they don't currently have, but would be complementary to purchases they've made in the past?"

If someone is a very profitable customer to you, it usually means that they like doing business with you, need a lot of what you have to offer, trust you, and often think of you as the "go-to" solution for problems related to your area of service and expertise.

So if you have a good recommendation that could help bring them value to their life, and is a perfect fit for something you've offered them in the past, you're likely to meet with success.

Here's how you can maximize your efforts. Start with your top 20 customers. What you want to do is write a PERSONAL letter to each of them. Start with talking about how you were analyzing your past records and noticed that they have been a very good customer, and that you value their business. Then say you also noticed something that may be a benefit, and since they've been a good customer, you're going to give them a special deal next time they come into the store and purchase something for you. Give them specific examples, such as...

"I noticed you purchased X from us. Well a new product we just got rights to complements X perfectly, so if you come in within the next 2 weeks I can give you a special deal of 40% off the shelf price. This is just my way of saying thanks for being such a valuable customer."

Another strategy to consider is the referral strategy. Think about this: people typically hang around others who share their same values and beliefs. This is a perfect way to attract new customers who are likely to be just as profitable as your past "most profitable customers".

In this case, you'd send your best customers a letter, and let them know that you're making them a "valued customer special offer" if they recommend someone to your business, and you'll give their referrals a "preferred VIP discount" or "preferred VIP treatment", since they came from a highly valued source.

People love to refer when this is the case. It makes them look good in front of their friends, and a lot of people get value in that. It's also great for you, because word of mouth advertising is some of the best advertising there is. Also, if you can just get these referrals into the door and have them start a buying relationship with you, chances are they will continue to buy from you in the future. Thus you will get more than just a one-off purchase, you may get a customer for life with a high lifetime value.

The Referral Marketing Goldmine

THE POWER OF "WORD OF MOUTH"

Referrals are the cheapest, yet the most effective marketing in the world.

The idea is that you should be generating a large portion of your new customers by marketing to existing customers.

There are several reasons why this is smart to do. First, quality attracts quality. Psychologists say that you are basically a combination of your five closest friends. In other words, people will refer people who are similar to them.

So if you have a big spender, then guess what? They'll probably refer other big spenders. Every good customer should be actively pursued for a referral because they'll usually generate other customers of equal quality and value.

Also, marketing is usually met with skepticism. That's because you are often tooting your horn. But what if some one else was tooting your horn for you?

Know this – people are more likely to believe in you if someone else endorses your quality than if you yourself brag about your own qualities.

What you're really doing is leveraging off of someone else's credibility. People who take the recommendations of their friends are now coming to you with a preconceived notion that you're *already* quality – before you even have to open your mouth.

Finally, word of mouth marketing is target marketing. Basically, you're only going to be getting people who already are in the market for what you're offering. Mass marketing does not have this effect. If you run an ad on television, you're getting everybody who watches TV.

But with referral marketing, you're pretty much *only* getting people who are already great matches to your products or services. This means your closing rate will go up without having to learn one single bit of salesmanship. You're just getting people who are already more likely to say "yes" before they even enter into the store.

Okay, know my rule of thumb when it comes to referral marketing – every good customer should get three direct chances to refer someone else to you.

I have found in order to get the best results, you have to ask someone three times to make a referral on your behalf. If you do nothing else, you should do this.

However, to really make it effective, there are two more things you need to do: make it easy for them to refer, and make it worthwhile to refer. I'm going to show you how to do all of this and more, as I outline what I have found time and time again to be a profit pulling monster when it comes to referral systems.

THE REFERRAL SYSTEM, STEP BY STEP

First, get your metrics in order. How much money can you afford to spend on marketing for next month? Whatever it is, devote the largest portion of it to your referral marketing. So step one, find your budget.

Now, the specific plan I'm going to lay out for you is going to cost around $8 per person to perform. So if you have a budget of $800 for marketing, then you can reach 100 people.

Start small and scale up – that's my advice. Don't spend too much upfront until you get back some reliable figures, and you can do some testing. Since this is a system, every dollar you spend will be tracked and traced back to determine the return on investment.

Here's how it works. Someone comes in and buys from you. Immediately the next day, you send them out a letter in the mail. You thank them, ask for the referral, make it easy for them to refer, and then make it worth their while.

The most important part here is that it's in *their* best interest to refer others to you. For that to happen, first and foremost you must have provided quality and value. So I'm going to assume you're performing good service and living up to your end of the deal.

Second, gifts work wonders. My favorite kind of gifts are those that either cost me nothing or very little, but have a huge perception of value. Without a doubt, there is one gift I can consistently create for basically nothing, and it always does the trick.

Coupon Books

It works like this – you go around to different business owners and tell them that you want to make sure your customers shop locally. As a thank you gift for your customers, you'd like to give them coupons or special offers from other local merchants, so you're providing your customers with value, and also keeping business local.

Then you simply ask them if they have any coupons or anything they'd like to contribute to your "customer gift book".

Almost every business owner you talk to will take you up on this. Why? Well, most businesses are not good at marketing, and to make up for it they always have a special going on, or are willing to do anything if it means getting a few more customers in the store.

Besides, you only need to get like 15 or 20 different coupons anyway to make a great gift book. You can get this all done in a few hours.

So now you have a great gift that you can give to anybody who sends a referral your way. How much did it cost you? Just the cost to print up the coupons and mail them. So you just made a gift of high perceived value (everybody loves coupons!) that costs you about $1 to create and a few hours of sweat equity, thus, it's worth their while.

Now let's take a look at what the first referral letter should look like:

Dear Jane Customer,

The other day you made a purchase from our store, and we just wanted to say thank you from the bottom of our hearts for doing business with us. If there is anything you ever need in the future, please do not hesitate to call us up and ask. We'll see what we can do!

You may not know it, but the lifeline of our business comes from referrals. If you happen to know anyone else who could use our services, I'd be extremely happy to sit down and talk with them to see if we might be able to help them in any way.

And, if it so happens that the person you refer becomes our customer, then as a token of my appreciation I will send you my special "valued customer gift book", which has a total of over $250 off coupons for discounts from local business of all kinds!

I'll give the same gift to your friend as well.

It's really easy to refer someone to us. I've enclosed two of my business cards with your name written on the back of them. Just give them to anyone who you think could use our services. Just have them present the business card when they come in, so we know it was you that referred them!

Anyway, I just wanted to say thanks again for deciding to go with us!

Thanks,
Joe Business Owner

There is a lot of psychology that is going on in this first letter that I don't want you to miss.

First, it's personal and it's sincere. How many businesses have you bought something from in the last sixty days that sent you a personal thank you letter in the mail?

Hmmm... Maybe 1 or 2 you say?

So imagine what kind of impact that your letter has when it lands in your customer's mailbox. Big impact. It says you care. Do you know why most people leave a service provider?

A few die. Some move away. Others leave because of an unresolved complaint. A handful will be stolen away by a competitor. Now add all those up, and guess what?

It usually only comes to 32% of all total customers who leave you. So what about the other 68%?

They leave simply because you never have taken the time to recognize them as something more than a customer.

Pop quiz – If you had an unresolved complaint, a direct competitor in your store trying to steal your customer, or the opportunity to let someone who purchased from you know you care... and you can only choose one option... which one should you choose?

You better choose the third option because roughly only 9% leave because of competition, and only 14% leave because of unresolved complaints.

If you do nothing else but keep in contact with your past customers and treat them as your friends and acknowledge them once in a while, you'll be putting the "golden handcuffs" on 2/3 of your customers, so you can keep selling to them again and again.

If you get nothing else out of the referral letter, you will get that personal communication that will separate you from 90% of all businesses, and almost every single one of your competitors.

The second thing that letter does is conveys your expectations. You expect all of your customers to refer. Most people don't refer simply because they don't know you want them to refer. In fact, I've had customers come up and tell my clients -- "Heck, I thought you already had enough customers. I didn't know you could take on more..."

You should've seen that business owner slap his forehead.

Once people know that you want them to refer, you automatically increase the chances they *will* refer, even if it isn't immediate. Again, I've had people hold on to business cards for two or three years before they gave one to someone else.

Also, notice the casual tone of the letter. People prefer doing business with friends, and not faceless corporations.

Finally, it shows you care. The above letter basically says, "Hey, I know you're busy and I know you've got to look out for your own self interests. That's why I've gone the extra mile to make it in your own self interest to refer me."

Ideally, you don't want to take the above letter word for word. You want to fill in "our services" with your actual services and so forth. But I give you permission to take most of the above verbatim and use it.

But don't stop there. After the first letter is sent out, wait 10-15 days, if you haven't gotten a referral from them yet, then send them letter two:

Dear Jane Customer,

A few weeks ago I sent you a letter thanking you for your purchase. I hope you got everything you wanted out of it and more. Remember – if you ever need help with anything, I'm only a phone call away.

We've also sent out several "customer gift books" in the last few weeks to our valued customers who referred one of their friends to us.

I know things can get busy, and sometimes stuff can get misplaced in the shuffle. To make sure you don't miss out on your own special customer gift book, I've sent you two more business cards with your name on the back – just in case you misplaced the last two I sent you.

Just give those to a friend in need, if you think we can help them, and we'll mail you your "customer gift book" pronto!

Once again, I just wanted to say thanks for being our customer, and we hope that we can continue to provide you with more service in the years to come.

Thanks,

Joe Business Owner

Here's what I know about marketing – one-shot advertising is not very effective. It's not that people don't want to act on your offers. A lot of them do. What happens is that the day to day details take over, and what they intend on doing ends up getting pushed to the back of their mind.

What this letter does is thank them again, puts you in front of them again, and basically let's them off the hook – hey, it wasn't their fault. You know they're busy people!

Also, it gives you another excuse to send them two more business cards. It also offers some social proof "hey, everybody else is referring".

Every time we track these campaigns, we usually find something like this – we get 3% to refer off the first letter. We get 4% to refer off the second letter, and we get 2% to refer off the third. In any case, all mailings are profitable.

Now think – if we just stopped after the first time, we'd get a 3% response. But instead we got a 9% response! In most scenarios, it almost always plays out that the second letter will work the best. Who knows why – it just does.

Now those who didn't respond to letter number one, and don't respond to letter number two, will get, after 10-15 more days, the third and last letter:

Dear Jane Customer,

Hope everything is going great for you! The reason I'm writing to you today is because I had a few "customer gift books" left over and didn't want them to go to waste.

I had one specifically set aside for you, so I have enclosed it with this letter. It is just our way of saying thanks for being a great customer.

Also, just in case you lost the last cards in the laundry or something, I've put in two more business cards with your name on the back.

Just pass them on to a friend if they're ever in need of any of the services that we offer...We'll make sure to treat them right.

Thanks!

Joe Business Man

Now, I don't want you to confuse the technique with the strategy. This works because:

- It puts you in front of them 3 times.

- It conveys the expectation that they will refer.

- It is personal and friendly.

- It is easy to do.

- It is in their own best interest.

You don't have to do the coupon gift book. Sometimes I'll just purchase tickets for a special upcoming local event, or even complimentary dinners at a good restaurant.

Lastly, a few more pointers – make your letters look like personal letters. This means, when you design the layout, don't put some fancy "brochure" feel into it. Just picture how you'd design the letter if you were going to sit down and write someone a personal note from a typewriter.

Also, when you get this system in place, you'll get some numbers. You might find for every 5 customers you do this for, you get 1 referral in the next 30 days. Okay, do that math – let's say your average sale netted you $600 in profit.

And let's say when you deduct all marketing expenses for creating and mailing the letters, it cost you $100. That's a 6 to 1 return on investment! Try getting that with other types of advertising.

This type of marketing also allows you to test. What would happen if you altered the gift? You can literally test every element you want, and know what is working and what isn't working. This means you can figure out the exact combination of steps for getting the greatest return on investment.

How to Tear Down Customer Resistance

How many of the people who walk into your business, or who take an interest in your products and services, end up going ahead with a purchase? In sales, this is called a closing rate.

To manage something, you first have to measure it. That way you know where it's at, so you know what you need to do to improve it.

So here's a simple question you need to have an answer to – if 10 prospects are interested in doing business with you, on average how many out of those 10 end up doing business with you?

The percentage itself isn't important. In stores with a lot of traffic, you can do 1 out of 10 and be fine. I have a website where I do 1 out of 100, and it's good enough for me to make a great return on investment, because it takes hardly any time or effort. In some businesses, you need 5 out of 10 just to have a chance at making a profit.

What *is* important is knowing how to improve your percentages to a more "acceptable" range. So if you get 5 out of 10, do the math and see how much more you'd make if you got 6 out of 10. Since they're already coming in the door, most of the work is done. You're just looking for those "little things" to get more people converted into customers.

There are a lot of different ways to improve your closing rate, and some are more complicated than others. I always look for the "80/20" factor in any given task. In other words I'm looking for that one or two key things that will make most of the difference between someone purchasing from you or not. Here's some insight to help you discover that "vital one fact" that gives you a majority of your results.

Do you know what three things are *required* before a prospect becomes a customer? Knowing this will give you the answer you need. Here are the three things that are needed:

First, they have to want what you offer.

Second, they have to have money to purchase it.

Third, they have to believe that you'll actually come through on your end of the deal.

The more inclined they are to already want what you have, the easier it is to sell to them. The more money they have set aside for making consumer purchases, the easier it to the sell to them. The more they believe that you actually will deliver on your offer, the easier it is to sell to them.

I have before me a phone book with yellow page ads. I'm going to flip through it and quote some phrases. Here's are just a few (and the thoughts) :

- **"Dependable & Quality Service"**

  And here's what your typical savvy potential customer is thinking:

  "Oh yeah!? Says who?"

- **"Value, Service & Convenience"**

  This description is meaningless, and everybody knows it...They're thinking:

  "Prove It!"

- **"Friendly service"**

  Once again, consumers have heard this all before, and they are thinking:

  "Yeah, right!

In other words, these are hollow phrases of puffery that everybody uses. It's so easy to say those things, and so saying those things mean very little. I've actually called a business whose yellow page ad said "friendly service" only to be treated rudely by the receptionist who answered the phone. Guess someone forgot to tell her!

So how do you go beyond mere puffery and actually prove your case that you are friendlier, more valuable, offer better service and are more dependable than every other option they have available?

Well, I'll share with you one simple way to do this that will drastically differentiate you from every competitor, both direct and indirect. As a bonus, it's also very simple to do, is extremely cost effective and when compiled, can be used in a variety of different outlets and mediums. What I'm talking about is customer testimonials.

THE SELLING POWER OF TESTIMONIALS

If you want to increase your closing rates without resorting to any fancy tricks or learning a bunch of new skills, just start being an avid collector of testimonials.

I don't care what anyone else says, they work.

Consider this – what if I told you I was the greatest marketing consultant of all time? Would you really believe me? What if your friend called you up and told you I was the greatest marketing consultant? Then you *might* believe it.

But what if your lawyer, your doctor, your mother, your children's principal, the head of your trade association and the guy you buy bell peppers from at the local farmer's market told you I was the greatest marketing consultant of all time?

I bet you'd be really interested in sitting down and having a talk with me, wouldn't you? You'd probably think a great deal more of me than from me just calling you up and bragging about my skills.

This is such a simple principle, it makes me wonder – why don't *all* businesses use testimonials? I don't know why. I think it should be a requirement of doing business personally. That is because, when it comes to raising your closing rates, it makes all the difference.

Now let me show you when, where and how to get these killer testimonials that will increase the believability of your offers.

HOW TO BECOME AN AVID TESTIMONIAL COLLECTOR

If you go looking for opportunities to get testimonials, you'll find it's easy to begin collecting them.

The best opportunity is when your customer is "in heat". What I mean by this is that you've just done something that has "wowed" them. They might come in to pay their bill and say "I can't believe what a wonderful service you did. It's better than the last five people I've gone to!"

This is your chance! You say: "Thanks! Would it be okay if I shared your story with others who might be interested in our services as well? It really helps us better serve our clients!"

Or, you can say: "Thanks. Would it be okay if I wrote down what you just said and shared it with others? It would mean a lot to me!" Then just write down really quickly what was said, and have them approve it.

Or you can simply say: "Thanks. Did you know that one of the best ways we get good clients just like you is sharing the success stories of our past clients? Would it be okay if we quoted you in some of our marketing and sales communications?"

Don't make it harder than it has to be. The main process is – get them when they're in a good mood. Ask if you can have their permission to quote them and share their story. Then get their testimonial. That's it.

Also, it's smart if you ask them if you can share their name with others as well, just to be on the safe side.

If you do nothing else, just collect testimonials from customers who are in heat and have just expressed how appreciative they are of you and your services.

Another good time is when you "save the day". Did you do something for a customer that was out of the ordinary? Maybe you made a house call at 8:30 at night to fix an emergency, free of charge. Or perhaps they wanted something that was supposedly discontinued, but you went the extra mile and tracked down what they were looking for.

Anytime you save the day, just ask them for a testimonial. In fact, I intentionally look for opportunities to save the day, because it serves in my self interest. If I go the extra mile, then I know they'll give me one heck of a testimonial!

Once you get good at the first two, consider sending out a customer survey once in a while. Have them answer a few key questions. Then, retype those answers up in a letter form, and ask them to sign off on it as a testimonial that you can share with others.

There are more aggressive ways to get testimonials, and I would encourage you to be aggressive about getting them, especially after you've gotten the knack for getting the low hanging fruit. Once you get used to asking your "in heat customers" and those who you've "saved the day for", experiment with actively seeking out testimonials to further prove your case.

HOW TO USE TESTIMONIALS FOR MAXIMUM EFFECT

I'm going to give you some examples that you can literally knock off and use in your own business, and also that you can use to brainstorm your own ideas from.

Let's return to the yellow book example. Instead of the typical puffery, your ad might include something that says:

"Look, any business can say that they care about the customer and that they are dependable and have high quality service. Instead of us touting our own horn, maybe you'd rather hear it from some of our customers themselves. Just call our 'satisfied customer hot line' to hear a pre-recorded message of what our customers think about our services..."

You know how much a voice mail account costs? About $4 a month. For $4 a month, you can have a recording of your best customers. How do you get these recording?

Perhaps you have your sales reps call your customers a few days after the sale. Explain to the customer that for quality issues, would it be okay if you recorded the call? This can be done inexpensively with a digital phone recorder that costs less than $50, or through an online service for about $10 a month.

Then, ask them what their thoughts were on the service or for the product. At the end, ask them if it would be okay if you shared their thoughts with others who might be interested in the products or services.

That's just one way to get your testimonials recorded. There are others.

Now you have a tool – you have people talking about how good you are. You can put this prerecorded message into all of your marketing communications! Your believability goes through the roof.

Here's something else you might want to consider – gathering up a "testimonial book".

Do you know ANY salesperson who has a testimonial book? Hmm... Wouldn't that distinguish you from every other competitor out there? I think it would... and in a good way.

Let's say you really went the extra mile and totally knock it out of the park for a customer. They were so happy they called you up and thanked you personally, and said they were so impressed with you and that you went above and beyond the call of duty.

Well how about this – you ask them if it would be okay to feature them as a "case study" in your next advertisement. Then you could write an advertisement that looks like an article, where you simply tell the story of what you did for this customer. This type of advertisement is about a million times more effective than the "BUY MY PRODUCT!" advertisements you currently see everywhere.

At the very least, you should include some testimonials in your advertising, just to enhance your claims.

One person I knew went as far as recording on video his customer testimonials. Then, when someone didn't purchase the first time they came into his store, five days later they'd get the video in the mail that contained all these wonderful customer testimonials.

Needless to say, a lot of people came back and ended up purchasing who otherwise would not have.

THE ANATOMY OF A GOOD
TESTIMONIAL

Now, some people have tried testimonials and have told me that they don't work. Well, it reminds me of my Dad telling me five years ago that his DVD player didn't work. I asked him -- "Did you plug it in?"

Oops!

Testimonials are like anything else – if you do them poorly then they probably won't work. In order to do them right, you must know what a good testimonial looks like.

Here's a bad testimonial:

"You did a good job!"

Here's a killer testimonial:

"You responded to our call and were at our house in 7 minutes. The last guys took 2 hours. Not only that, you helped us save 13% off the cost. Thanks a bunch!" -- Jason Happypants, Fire Fighter, Fresno, CA

The difference is obvious. Bad testimonials are bland and really don't say anything. Good testimonials are specific, and give you hard facts. I love it when someone says to me: "I read your book on Thursday, and by Saturday morning I did one thing I learned on page 8 that resulted in me making $15,867.13 in profit by the following Tuesday. You're a genius!".

That's a far better testimonial than "your ideas helped me make more money".

Not only is specificity needed, but it's good to have a name, location and occupation. Otherwise people will think that maybe you're just making up the testimonials yourself, even though that is illegal. (Which is why audio and video testimonials are the best)

Also, there are other things that can influence your testimonials. What's better — five testimonials featured in your ads from white males aged 43 and over, or a mix of ages, races and both males and females?

Well, it depends. If your product targets white males that are 43 years old, then it's a good idea.

If it targets a wide variety of audiences, then you want testimonials from a wide variety of people.

Lastly, as humans we're hardwired by nature to trust authority. That's why testimonials from scientists, doctors, nurses, fire fighters, and other esteemed positions tend to have more pull than regular testimonials. Just think how much more credible a testimonial is from a rocket scientist than a "sanitary enginer".

So set a plan – come up with the different ways you're going to capture and use testimonials, and make sure everybody in your business starts to become a testimonial collector. It's one of the easiest ways to increase your sales closing percentage.

The *Right* Way to Place Yellow Page Ads

I'm going to preface this chapter by saying I know I knock Yellow Page ads a lot. I'm really not a big fan. But, they do serve their purpose and some folks insist on using them, so these are the best practices I have found.

Have you noticed that 95% of Yellow Page ads look the same? There's a problem with going with the "norm" -- you get normal results.

With your business and livelihood on the line, I hope you're not content with average results, especially when extraordinary results are so easy to get with Yellow Pages. You only need to do a few simple things.

The first thing you have to understand is what people are looking for when they open up the yellow pages. Some people are looking for SPECIFIC contact information. They already have a service provider in mind. It's hard to get those people.

But the good news is when most people open up the Yellow Pages, they are looking for information *to help them find the best business to contact* that will give them the solution they desire.

And here's what most consumers want: They want a good deal, they want to go with someone who is able to understand their needs and lead them to the best solution, and they want to deal with as little headaches, delays and customer service problems as possible.

Now, flip open your yellow pages and see if any of the ads address those points, and you'll find hardly any do so adequately.

Good. That will make it much easier for you.

I'm going to show you how to create a simple yellow page ad that will make people believe that if they contact you or go into your store, that they are going to get the best solution for their dollars, and it's going to be easy and convenient to deal with you, and that you're the best choice for all of their options.

If you can pull that off, you're going to get the lion's share of Yellow Page customers in your industry.

THE MOST IMPORTANT PART OF YOUR AD

The world's best ad is no better than the world's worst ad if no one sees it. So the first job your Yellow Page ad must do is get the attention of the people who are best matched to take advantage of the services and products that you offer.

The easiest way to do that is with a good attention-getting headline.

To understand what a good headline looks like, first let's look at some bad headlines. I went through my own local Yellow Pages, and found these headlines:

"The Blind Factory"

"Cyclists Serving Cyclists"

"Wet Basement or Crawl Space"

"Quality Construction"

"Professional Muffler, Inc"

"Old Fashioned Values, Including Our Own People Doing the Work"

These are all terrible headlines. First, almost all of them talk about the service provider, and not the person who is looking at the ad. Talk about selfish and self-centered!

Second, none of them promise any benefit to the person... none of them get the person reading excited... and most are nothing more than the name of the company.

Your headline is the most important part of your yellow page ad so you need to do better. Ideally, you want a headline that promises a benefit to the reader, and is written to grab the attention of a certain large segment of the population who is best matched for the goods and services you provide.

Let's look at the first one -- "The Blind Factory". How could this one be improved? Here is a good headline that I have found gets great results... "The 6 Mistakes Most People Make When They Purchase Blinds For Their Home...".

Or... "Warning: Don't Buy Any Blinds Until You Read This...". Or Even "How to Get the Best Blinds For You Home in 48 Hours Or Less, Guaranteed!".

Notice the difference with these headlines? First, they focus on the consumer. Second, they promise a huge benefit. Third, they call out a certain portion of the general population – in this case, people who are looking to purchase blinds, who want to get a good deal, want ease of service, or want to make sure they don't commit a mistake when buying blinds.

Once you have a good headline, the ad practically writes itself. For example, let's return to the headline: "The 6 Mistakes People Make When They Purchase Blinds for Their Home". You would then come up with 6 mistakes that you find people tend to make if they don't have an expert to help them select their product. And then, after you introduce each mistake, explain how that mistake can be avoided if they come into your store.

Remember, people who open up the Yellow Page ads are generally looking for *information to help them make the best decision* on who to buy from. So typically the person who provides the most information wins... and it helps if that information is all beneficial to the reader.

But if you look at the typical Yellow Page ad, it has 50 words or less, and is usually filled with puffery. For example, I always see "The customer comes first". And I always say – prove it!

Which leads us to the second biggest point about writing effective Yellow Pages ads: making powerful, unique claims to demonstrate that you're better than any other solution that's available in the Yellow Pages.

So how can you make a unique claim that demonstrates that "the customer comes first". Here's a technique that's been used to great effect. The first thing you do is contact some of your past satisfied customers. Then, you ask them to write a quick one paragraph testimonial about what they liked most about dealing with you. (It's easy to do this with the right strategy).

Then, you put all those testimonials on a website. Now, in your ad you can say, "You can even read what 117 satisfied customers had to say about our great products at..." and then put the website address in there.

Now, most people looking at the ad WON'T go to page and read it. But it will have the effect of demonstrating to them that not only does the customer come first, but you have 117 of your own customers who say that you DO put them first. You'll be the only ad in your category that can claim that, so in people's minds you'll be the preferred source if customer service is their main priority.

At any rate, your ad should contain at least one dramatic example of proof to validate your claims. It's best if you have specific numbers or facts to verify it, testimonials to show and other powerful ways to demonstrate that you offer great service and goods.

For example, you can do much better than merely stating something like "In business since 1972!" My first reaction when I see this statement is "So what?"

The fact is, I know a lot of bad companies that have stayed in business for decades. Instead, you can say "We've successfully helped over 10,678 clients in [city name] find the right blinds for their home."

So first come up with a powerful headline. Then, expand on that headline in your ad, and also throw in at least one dramatic example of proof to validate your claims.

Now you only have to do one final thing.

HAVE AN OFFER AND A "CALL TO ACTION"

Every single ad you write should have an offer and a call-to-action to accept that offer. A call to action means that you tell them exactly what they should do after reading the ad.

Let me start with the best call to action, although it's also the most complicated one to set up.

What you ideally want is a continuing relationship with people who are interested in doing business with you, so if they are hesitant initially, further communication can get them in the door.

The best way to do that is to offer something free to the user if they contact you. Here's a simple way to do that. Let's go back to the Blinds example.

The first thing you'd want to do is sit down and write a little 6-8 page report on "How to Pick The Most Beautiful Blinds For You Home On A Shoe-string Budget" or something like that.

Then just give them the best tips for getting the most value from their purchase.

What you're going to want to do next is take that report (written on a computer) and export it as a PDF (you can do this for free with OpenOffice, which you can download on the internet).

Then, you're going to want to set up an "autoresponder" account at aweber.com. This allows you to have people sign up for an email list, so you can send them emails in the future.

Then, if they sign up for your list, they will automatically be delivered your free digital report on "How to Pick The Most Beautiful Blinds For You Home On A Shoe-string Budget." Not only that, you can use your autoresponder to send a few follow up messages automatically at certain intervals to anyone who signs up.

Then in your Yellow Page ad you say, "If you'd like to get our free report on "How to Pick The

Most Beautiful Blinds For You Home On A Shoe-string Budget", then just go to www.your websiteaddress.com". This drives them to a page that explains that in order to get the report they just have to enter in their name and email into the form. (the form will be created automatically for you if you use Aweber.)

Of course, in the report you're going to want to put your contact information so if they read it they can easily contact you and become your customer.

This is by far the best strategy but also the most complex. A simple strategy is to make a "Yellow Page ad only" offer. In this case you say, "If you call us today to schedule an appointment, and mention that you are calling because of the Yellow Page ad, we'll give a 10% off Yellow Page 'special deal".

In any case, you're enticing them to respond to your ad.

If you do all of the things in this report, then you're going to have an ad that is dramatically different than everyone else's which will allow you to get dramatically better results!

Getting Online And Where To Start

Up until now we've been talking about how to improve your offline business, marketing strategies and the importance of getting online. But where should you start online? Facebook? Twitter? Building a website? Start a Blog? Linked-In? Mobile Marketing?

The answer might scare you a bit, but I always suggest: all of the above!

Everything mentioned above will create a community that will take your offline business to a whole new level. I'm purposely targeting this chapter to you offline, brick and mortar folks because most of the onliners already know this. Now, whether they've implemented any of it or not is an entirely different subject.

I would recommend that you attack this in a certain order though, and that order starts with mobile local marketing. Here are just a few of the reasons I think Mobile Marketing is so important:

-In 2008 according to a Piper Jaffray research paper, 30 percent of all search engine queries contained a city, state or zip code. (and that was back in 2008!) For example, rather than searching for a "Dentist", somebody in Boca Raton, Fl. would search for a "Dentist in Boca Raton". That's what we call a city specific search term or local marketing search term.

- In 2010, that number is estimated to be closer to the 65 to 70 percent range.

- Apple, no longer refer to themselves as a computer or software company, they are now a Mobile Company.

- There are over 60 billion searches per month on Google alone, of those 6 billion contain local terms.

- Twitter gets 19 million searches a day! 5 percent of those contain local search terms.

- As of May 2010, it was estimated that 65,000 new Android devices were sold per day! That's not counting iphones or iPads, just Android devices.

- Google spent $750 million to acquire Admob, one of the largest advertising networks that specializes in delivering ads to mobile devices. (Apple also bid to acquire Admob and was outbid by Google. Shortly thereafter, they created their own mobile advertising platform, iAd)

- Millions of websites have gone "Mobile Friendly" in their design. (Mobile Facebook users have reached (and surpassed) 150 million)

- The "average" person is said to look at their mobile phone 45 times a day. (I think it's more than that, it is for me anyway)

Wow, can you see a trend here?

Companies, both big and small, are investing their time and efforts into expanding the "mobile device" market and the more this occurs, the more opportunity you have to get in front of your targeted audience.

Yellow pages and newspapers are on their way out, as a matter of fact I can't remember when I last laid eyes on one of those big yellow books.

Have you heard of Google Places and Google Maps? If the above stats didn't impress you much, the power of this should blow your mind. Let me paint a picture for you, consider the following scenario:

Jennifer is driving down the street, your street, the same street that your Discount Womens clothing store is on. As coincidence would have it, Jennifer is in the mood for some light shopping before her 2 pm meeting. While she's at the light, Jen pulls out her smartphone and quickly types in "Womens Clothing", within seconds a Google map appears on her phone highlighting all of the Womens clothing stores within a five mile radius.

Are you on that map? Or does Jen drive right by your store heading to one that is instead?

Conservatively, that exact scenario, with the difference being the type of business and Jen's name, happens all the time. Depending on the town, type of business and poularity of the street, it may happen up to 100 times a day.

How much difference would it make to your bottomline if you received ten new customers a day from mobile marketing?

And this is the most basic of scenarios; we haven't even gotten to the good stuff yet.

Now, imagine the same scenario above, only this time factor in some variables that are not only possible, but likely, if you've embraced local mobile marketing.

Back to Jen. After Jen conducts her search, still at the light, and finds a list of stores and a map, which took her about 15 to 20 seconds, she clicks on the first bubble on the map, because you've hired a top notch mobile marketing consultant, that bubble happens to be yours. Great so far, but if all that pops up is the address to your store, what's the guarantee that she'll choose you over on of the other bubbles? Well, what if one of the following occurs when she clicks on your bubble:

- A coupon pops up on her phone offering an instant 10 to 20 percent savings if she comes in right now!

- A page pops up talking about the latest designs or Discount specials available today only!

- A message pops up saying "Hey, we just brewed a fresh pot of coffee, stop by and have a free cup while shopping!"

etc.

Are you beginning to see the power of mobile marketing?

What if you took it a step further by offering her an instant 25 percent savings on anything purchased today in return for her email address or better yet, her phone number? Then you could keep her as a customer for life by adding her to your weekly email or text newsletter and send her updates and specials once or twice a week via email or text message.

Did you know, text messages are opened 95 percent of the time as opposed to emails which are only opened on average 3 to 5 percent of the time? I've thrown alot of stats at you, but this one is worth mentioning again. 95 percent of all text messages are opened. Oh, and they're opened within 2 to 3 minutes of being received.

I'm going to end this chapter here, Not because there isn't anything more to say about mobile marketing, quite the opposite, but because I think you should really take a few minutes before heading to the next chapter and wrap your head around the power of that last paragraph. In light of today's attention deficit society, that one was a doozy.

I have three words for you:

Mobile, Local, Marketing.

Find someone good at it and hire them, period.

Free Report:

I've Put Together A Free Guide To Mobile Marketing For You, You Can Get It Here:

http://IsYourBusinessGoogleable.com/Mobile-Marketing-Guide

What About Facebook And Is It Worth My Time?

Is Facebook worth my time as a small business owner? That's by far the most common question I get and I'm pretty sure I get asked that at least once a day.

The short and sweet answer is a resounding:

YES

But there are several ways to go about creating a facebook presense online for a small business specifically. If you research the subject on the net, reading article after article, you'll just get overwhelmed and dissapointed. That's the point at which most of my clients simply determine that they DON'T have enought time to do it right. But that should not be the case.

Granted, setting up a facebook page for a business and getting started can seem overwhelming and may require some technical skills. Notice I said a page and not a profile. Profiles are for personal use, you would set up a profile for yourself to interact with family and friends. But, for a business, you would set up a fan page. As the term suggests, the purpose of this page is to gather fans.

If, for some reason or another, you think that your business might not be a right fit for a Facebook fan page, consider this: there are over 600 million facebook users. Everything and everywhere is covered. There are more people logging in to Facebook everyday than Google. Yes, it's actually more popular than Google.

So, we've established that it's worth your time, but how do you go about setting it up?

There's a mistake 90 percent of small business owners make right off the bat. They assume that because there are 600 million users, it must be really simple to set up. And, generally speaking they're right. For the general public, setting up a FB profile takes about 7 minutes, and it's dead easy to do. But you're not the general public, as a small business owner, you should know that by now.

You're unique, you offer a service better than anyone else, you care about your customers more, you interact with them on a deeper level, your solution to their problem is genuine, you're fair and service oriented. Right? That's the whole idea of social marketing, to get in front of your prospects where they are, but without interfering with them, get that right and your business will flourish because of it. Get that wrong, and you will reap no benefit from your efforts.

That's why setting up your Facebook fan page the right way from the start, is critically important for success. If you have the time and the tech skills required, it's not that difficult to do. There's no shortage of manuals and programs online to guide you. Do I recommend that route? No. I may be biased because it's my business to set you up the right way from the start, but that's not the reason I'm against it. I'm against it, because it takes me so much longer to correct errors and overcome mistakes that have been created because of it.

So just keep this in mind, whether you choose to set things up yourself, or hire a professional to do it for you. Small Business fan pages are different. They serve an entirely different purpose than a Profile or a fan page set up for, oh let's say... bungee jumping!

That shouldn't scare you off, it simply means you may need to hire someone to create a professional looking fan page that stands out from the rest and delivers your message to your target audience. Same way you would call a plumber to install a new toilet. Here's the good news, just like the toilet, once the fan page has been created, you no longer need the plumber to use it! You just need a daily plan, or strategy and you must stick to it.

Having said that, here's are ten reasons you need a strategy:

1. Everybody And Their Mom Is On Facebook

There are over six hundred milion reasons why your business should be on facebook, and every week thousands of new people join.

120 million+ of these users are based in the US, which is an important reason why your business

cannot ignore Facebook if you want to have a serious presence in the US.

2. Facebook Fans By More Of Your Stuff

A recent study done by Facebook calculated the value of each Facebook Fan.

FAcebook asked 4,000 fans of 20 of the top brands on Facebook about their spending habits, and found the following:

-Fans are 28 percent more likely than non-fans to continue using a specific brand.

-Fans are 41 percent more likely than non-fans to recommend a product they are a fan of to their friends.

-On average, fans spend an extra $71.84 per year on that brand that they would not otherwise spend, on products they describe themselves as fans of, compared to those who are not fans.

-68% of fans on Facebook say they are very likely to recommend a product (and in a sense 100% of Fans recommend the pages they have joined by displaying their fanship on Facebook)

-McDonald's saw the largest variability, with Fans reporting spending $159.79 more per-year than non-fans

-Oreo saw the lowest value with a difference of $28.52.

3. Facebook Pages Are Flexible

The Tabpress application is very flexible, and gives you the ability to create "Fan Only" content and create a custom Facebook Page.

The flexibility of micro-sites means that you can display several different pages of content all within a single tab. If you have multiple products or services, you could have a page for each.

4. Facebook Can Drive Serious Traffic To Your Site

Once you have built up a fan base for your business you can post status updates about your latest blog posts and company news, and these will drive traffic back to your website.

You can also add a link to your web page in your "info tab," and if you want it to have an omnipotent presence on your page you can link to your site in your info box.

If you have a blog you can import your posts automatically via the RSS Graffiti or Networked Blogs applications. I prefer to post my updates manually so that they can go out at the time for optimum engagement (posts made in the morning typically get more attention).

You can set it up so that your Facebook posts are instanly and automatically posted tp your Twiiter page as well.

5. The Average User Spends 55+ Minutes On The Site

This means that if you are on Facebook there is a good chance that people will find you organically, simply because they are browsing around.

Make it easy for people to find your page by giving your page a long title including some relevant keywords, rather than simply your brand name. The reason for this is because you will be able to connect with new fans who find you via facebook search.

A longer page title also means that every time someome engages on your page a longer link will be created in their news feed, linking back to their engagement, and this means that every linkback to your page within facebook is more likely to be clicked.

6. The Average Facebok User Has 130 Friends

Facebook recently revamped their "Find Friends" tool, making it easier for people to connect with their friends than ever.

This means that any friend who is a fan of your page has their fanship openly displayed to over 130 people, which will lead to organic fan growth over time.

Be sure to create a memorable profile picture so that people who see the thumbnail of your page on their friends wall are inclined to click.

7. The Average User Fans 2+ Pages Per Month

Contrary to popular belief, not everyone that visits your page becomes a fan. Many simply stop by, and leave, if there is no pressing reason for them to join up.

To increase your fanship conversion, make sure that your fan page has a call to action for users to "like" your fan page.

One way to increase your conversion is by creating a custom landing page with an arrow calling the visitor to take the action of clicking the "like" button.

8. The Average Fan Is Worth $136.38

Perhaps the most staggering metric derived from this study is that the cumulative value of a fan is $136.38, when brand spending, loyalty, recommendations, and media value are considered.

9. Facebook Fan Pages Are Found Favorably in Google's Search Results

Facebook Pages and Groups rank very well in Google, since they are typically a source of fresh content.

The main factor that will get you found is the title of your page, so be sure to pick a page title that is keyword rich.

10. Facebook Offers Great Analytics To Help You Learn More About Your Fans

Facebook Insights is an awesome tool for analyzing everything from your page engagement, to your demographics, to your fan growth (or loss).

Test different methods of engaging with your fan page from week to week and then check Insights to see what works the best in terms of driving engagement and new fan growth.

Different methods of engagement to post could include posting different media (videos, pictures, notes), or even simply posting different types of status updates. Questions tend to get more engagement than regular status updates, so they are worth experimenting with as well.

Those are some pretty compelling reasons to set up a fan page, and there's so many more.

The second most common question I am asked is: What do I do after I've had my page set up? How do I stay in touch with my fans? How do I interact with them? What's my strategy?

OK, that was more than one question, but it's usually asked just like that, all in one breath, with a look of panic on their face. But again, there's nothing to worry about. Interacting with your fans can be fun, educational, productive, entertaining and most importantly, profitable. You just need a strategy.

Strategies will differ from business to business and it's something you should discuss with whomever you've chosen to create your Fan page for you. Typically, the strategy will work synergistically with the call to action of the Fan page. I like to discuss the overall business strategy with my clients first to determine what it is they are trying to achieve and how the Fan page will best benefit both them and their clients.

But there are some some general rules you can follow, here are some best practices, tips and tricks to stick to:

1. Write a Compelling Profile

Writing a complete and perfect Facebook profile that builds trust with the quantity of information you are willing to share.

I know, I know, I've harped on the fact that you should build a Fan page for your business, and I stick to that, but that doesn't mean you can't create a profile for yourself first. And you absolutely should. Many times your customers will want to learn more about you before they join your fan page, this holds especially true when you are a small 1 or 2 person business, and even moreso if you are servicing a local area. Be honest in your rofile and post a happy picture :-)

2. Set Realistic Goals

Don't expect to get thousands of fans to your Facebook page within your first month, but set a realistic goal and try to make progress towards it every day.

Then if you hit something larger than you originally anticipated, you'll be pleasantly surprised. Whetever fans you are able to acquire will help fuel your growth as your existing fans share your content with their friends.

3. Make Time To Post

Cultivating a Facebook presence doesn't have to be a full-time job nor something that eats up all your free time.

Try to set aside an hour a day to work on your business's page, post updates, and communicate directly with customers and fans.

4. Learn As Much As You Can

Take notes based on your experiences with Facebook's pages and other business services.

You'll find just about anything you're curious to know within Facebook's official help center.

Make a habit of reading as much as you can about Facebook.

5. Do It Right The First Time

I recommend using a Professional to set up your Fan pages.

It is a one time fee, we charge typically about $500 for a custom design, graphics and strong call to action. The call to action of Fan pages is almost always getting the visitor to "Like" your page.

When looking for someone to set up your page, remember the old saying "You get what you pay for".

Most of my colleagues in the biz will charge any-where from $400 up to $1,000 for a Fan page. If you ask me, it's totally worth it, not because the pages created are great, which they are, but it's the "what you should do next" converation and the level of support a professional can give you that makes the difference.

6. Use A Strong Call To Action

Your Facebook page should feature a big and bold call to action. This will help many visitors to your page take the action you are looking for, clicking the "Like" button.

Redbull does a good job of a very clear call to action, if you are looking for a template to model. Search for the RedBull page in Facebook and have a looksee.

7. Create a Fan Page For Your Business, Not A Profile

I've beaten this to death, but...

Don't open a second account on the social network to make a profile for your business.

Not only does that go against Facebook's rules but it also moves you one degree of separation away from the people who are already on your personal friend list.

These folks are the first people you want to invite to become fans of your business's page.

Recently Facebook upgraded their Pages product and now you can post on other pages as your page.

8. Build Relationships

Send a thank-you message right after someone clicks "like" on your page, and make a point of responding to messages and wall posts within 24 hours.

Pay careful attention to whatever fans tell you on your page, and try to respond to their needs.

9. Invest Your Time Wisely

It's possible to promote your business on Facebook without spending anything.

At some point you might get the itch to buy advertising, which certainly helps but also presents the temptation to overspend.

You're better off starting out doing small test ads to see what kind of performance you get for your money, and then ramp up when you figure out which demographics and key words you want to target.

People have gotten pretty tired of spammy self-promotion, and if you are all about yourself people will unlike you.

Instead spend time building relationships around your brand and add value. If you do this well your fans will return the favor by clicking the "Like" button and sharing your valuable content more often.

This is another area where hiring a professional for a few bucks more makes a difference. If you're ready to start advertising, call the person you hired to create your fan page, likely they are very good and have experience in advertising on FB. Usually, for a small fee, typically a couple hundred bucks, they can spend a couple hours and show you the best practices for targetting your key audience and saving a ton of time and money in the process.

I can tell you from experience, my clients usually call me after they've blown about $500 on getting 2 or three likes! And the mistakes they've made are usually very small, but when your advertising to thousands and paying per click, it adds up fast.

10. Create Coupons And Promotions

Discounts for first-time customers really work toward generating repeat business.

But don't limit the promotions to the first time someone engages with your company, or they may lose interest.

Periodically put things on sale if you can, in order to keep people coming back. It is far easier to market to an existing customer than it is to go out and try to find a new one.

11.   Encourage Check-Ins

Wherever your business operates, that counts as a place on Facebook.

Make a point of checking in to your place of work every day you are there, even if you're operating out of a home office.

This will put your company's name into people's news feeds every time you punch in.

Typically, in marketing, it is said that the average consumer must see your name or offer 7 times before they remember you or take action. So stay in front of them and be consistent.

12.   Expand Your Network

Facebook has a powerful Find Friends feature that allows you to find friends from pretty much any email service you might use.

You can even import a contact file, and this will allow you to import friends from contact files from networks like Linkedin.

13.   Create a Group

Groups are for groups of people, whereas pages are open platforms for brands.

Facebook's new Groups product is powerful and distinct from the old groups product.

The most noticeable feature that sets it apart now is how it allows you to add friends without their consent.

Groups can be especially useful in closed format as a tool for internal communications within a business, or to segregate groups of people that are interested in specific products or services you offer.

14.   Check Out Facebook Ads

Facebook Ads are very powerful as they allow you to drill down and target a very specific demographic.

You can target ads directly at people of a specific age, 30 year olds for example, and then in the headline you could address them directly with a line like "Are you 30?"

Refer back to point 9 above. Contact a Pro when you're ready to Go :-)

15.   Update Facebook And Twitter At The Same Time

There are several different ways to update both Facebook and Twitter and by doing so you save yourself the step of posting the same content twice.

If you have a blog, you can actually post the content to your blog and using a plugin have it automatically update your Facebook Fan Page and Twitter simultaneously. Now that's a time saver!

Talk to your Fan page creator, they can most likely set this up for you as well. A typical charge for a blog with autoposting capabilities, depending on customization, could run anywhere from $300 to $1,000, it's a one time set up fee.

If you order multiple products at the same time you can usually save a substantial amount. I offer my clients packages based on their needs that typically saves them 40 to 50 percent off the a la carte price.

16.   Post Cool Status Updates

Make your profile work for your page by posting witty status updates that encourage your friends to engage with your business page.

Apply that same sense of wit to the goal of one post per day to your page's wall.

If you can phrase it as a question there is a good chance that will inspire responses from your community.

Interaction is the name of the game, if you can get your fans to respond, like or ccomment on your post, your winning.

17.   Add Video To Your Page

If you have a YouTube channel Involver makes it easy to integrate it with your Facebook Page with the Involver YouTube application. You can also create a custom page template and embed a video against any background you like but this will of course require technical skills.

Going back to point 15 above, you can post the video to your blog and again using a simple plugin, have it auto post to facebook. Twitter doesn't do video ;-)

18. Further Integrate Facebook With Your Website Or Blog

Integrating Facebook with your website by installing Facebook Like Buttons and a Like Box will allow your visitors to easily join your community and share the content on your site.

When a visitor to your site or blog clicks the like button on your site, they are automatically a fan on Facebook as well and all of their friends can see that they've liked you. Some will come to check out your site, and the cycle repeats. Viral marketing at it's finest.

19. Promote Your Facebook Page Just Like You Would Your Website

Twitter is a great place to spread the word about your Facebook page. If you are on Linkedin there is an opportunity to share as well. You can also write articles that discuss your products, always in a beneficial light for your customers and not in a self promotional way, and at the end of the article you could ask them to join your Facebook Fan page for more info, specials, promotions and coupons, not to mention your witty posts.

Using article disttribution services you can quickly submit your new article and link to your

Facebook page to several directories around the web. This will begin the syndication process of your article which will result in a perpetual stream of incoming links and fresh new fans.

20.   Use Facebook Insights

I know I mentioned this before, but this is something you should get used to doing. Just like you should install Google Analytics on your blogs and/or site(s) to see who's visiting, how they found you, what they looked at or were looking for and how long they stayed on your site, you should use Facebook Insights as well.

Facebook Insights is a powerful analytics dashboard that is built into every Facebook page and will give you detailed information about your fans that will help you interact with them, post to your wall and market products they are interested in.

This is something your "guy or gal in the biz" can show you and explain how to use the data collected.

That's all for the best practices, tips and tricks section.

This chapter went on for much longer that I thought it would, but I think we covered alot of ground.

I hope this convinced you that Facebook is a good idea, and not only a good diea but a necessary tool in today's connected society. The fact that 600 million users like Facebook is reason enough for you to make a page for you business.

If all of this is overwhelming and you're having a hard time finding someone to put this together for you, give me a call and we'll find a way to work something out. My contact info is on the back of the book :-)

Free Report:

I've Put Together A Free Guide To Facebook Marketing For You, You Can Get It Here:

http://IsYourBusinessGoogleable.com/Guide-To-Facebook

Analytics Are Key To Your Success

I wasn't going to include this chapter on analytics only because it will be a little too advanced for most that are still trying to wrap there head around setting up a blog, and may seem over-whelming. But it is something that is an absolute necessity and for me, it's what makes marketing online so much more exciting than offline.

Offline, traditional style marketing is almost im-possible to gauge and even in instances where you can gauge the effectiveness, it takes forever. In contrast, gauging the effectiveness of an online campaign is almost instantaneous. Where offline it may take a week to several weeks to determine if an ad was effective, online it usually takes a few hours and worst case scenario, a day. It's not un-common to start getting data feedback within minutes.

So, analytics are crucial to a successful online marketing strategy. Whether you're marketing for direct sales, brand marketing, building an email or phone number list, the outcome is the same: without the proper analytics in place to tell you which implemented strategies are working and which ones are not, you are wasting time and money.

And how can you expect to streamline and optimize any project, if you can't pinpoint deficiencies, inefficiency, and unresponsive components? Being able to analyze the results of any marketing plan is paramount. An efficient analytic system should be in place before any new project is executed. The initial results are vitally important and will act as a baseline for any alterations or improvements made to the overall marketing strategy.

If there is no analytic process installed right from the very start, there is no available data to measure if any new implementations or strategy changes have improved, diminished, or made no difference to the initial project. Flying blind is not a good business practice.

Okay, I hope I haven't freaked you out too much, I'm going to bring this right back down to earth.

Basically, you should be tracking the movements of your visitors to and from your site(s). This is another reason why it is important to have a website or blog that you direct all of your traffic to from all of your different marketing efforts. This is called funneling and it makes it much easier for tracking your visitors behavior and measuring succcessful versus failed marketing strategies.

Here are two identical marketing scenarios, one with analytics tracking and one without:

Marketing Scenario:

Let's say you own a clothing retail store and you decide to start implementing an online marketing strategy including a blog or website featuring your items for sale, social media marketing including a facebook fan page, twitter page and maybe some youtube videos, and some local marketing such as an optimized Google places listing and some local review sites such as Foursquare. By the way, this is a perfect package for online marketing.

You have all of that in place and you begin by posting some articles to your blog, making some great comments on your facebook page offering some specials to your fans, re-post the comments to twitter directing them back to your facebook page and upload a couple of compelling videos featuring your fashions to you tube. A healthy amount of effort no doubt.

Over the next few days you start getting more customers than usual. You're thrilled and you attribute this to your new online marketing strategy. But you're curious, "I wonder which one of the marketing methods brought these guys in. Was it the Facebook page? My Tweets? Those awesome YouTube videos? Or did they find me just driving by from the Google places listing? Maybe it was the cool reviews on Foursquare".

Here are the Answers Without Analytics:

"I don't know, so I will just continue doing everything blindly, but the curiosity is killing me!"

Here are the Answers With Analytics:

"I'll just take a quick look at my analytics stats. Wow, I received 45 new visitors to my blog today, 35 of them came from my YouTube videos, 5 from my facebook page, two from Google Search Results and three direct."

"So now I know my YouTube videos are killing it, I'm going to concentrate on adding 5 more videos this week! My FaceBook fan page could use a bit more compelling comments and maybe a less aggressive sell position and a more friendly community approach, my Tweeps(slang for Twitter followers) weren't too impressed with my comments either, I'll try a different approach there and see if that improves, and hey, 5 new potential customers from Google, Great!"

Which position would you rather be in?

Now, this was a very basic, but very realistic scenario. There are so many other marketing variables that could've been implemented and tracked as well, such as 1-800 numbers, autoresponder messages, article marketing, blog commenting, forum posting and hundreds of others.

Without analytics it would just be a mess and you'd never know what you were doing right or wrong.

There are several ways to implement analytics and tracking on your site(s), some are paid and some are free. I find the free ones work just as good as the paid ones, although some of the paid ones will offer a little deeper insight into your traffic and visitor behavior.

For now, let's focus on the best free system out there and the one I recommend and use the most.

Google Analytics

This isn't a lesson in installing and mastering Google Analytics per se, it's more of an outline to get you thinking about the possibilities and benefits of adding analytics to your site(s) and the importance of understanding your visitors behavior, reactions and patterns before, during and as they exit your site.

First off, installing Google Analytics, which we'll call GA from this point on, is super simple, here the basic setup.

Step 1. Sign up for a Google Account

Step 2. Go to the GA page here: *www.google.com/analytics/*

Step 3. Click "Access Analytics"

Step 4. Insert your URL (website address)

Step 5. Copy the code and paste it on your site where Google tells you too.

Your site is now being analyzed, your visitors tracked and data is being collected. Check back tomorrow and make sure everything is working.

Now let's talk about the basic stats you'll be able to analyze in your analytics back panel.

Site usage overview (Main > Dashboard)

7,555 Visits
Previous: 7,860 (-3.88%)

74.96% Bounce Rate
Previous: 75.66% (-0.93%)

14,915 Pageviews
Previous: 14,711 (+1.39%)

00:02:05 Avg. Time on Site
Previous: 00:01:52 (+11.87%)

1.97 Pages/Visit
Previous: 1.87 (+5.48%)

55.46% % New Visits
Previous: 57.44% (-3.45%)

Visits

Visits are the number of sessions that occur on your website. A visit is, as close as possible, one person who views one or more pages on the site. If the same person comes back, that's two visits.

More visits to a site equates, basically, to more "traffic" and, potentially, more people in general seeing the site. A visit count increasing means more sessions on the site which could indicate 1) more people returning to the site or 2) more new people on the site. Combining the change in visits with the change in percentage of new visits can give you an idea which of these scenarios is contributing the most. Month to month, you typically want this number to increase.

Pageviews

Pageviews are the number of pages on your site that were viewed. Generally, each link you click takes you to a new page. If, in one month, 1,000 people went to the homepage, clicked on an article, clicked on another article, and then went elsewhere, that month would have 3,000 page views.

Like visits, this is also a number that, generally, should be increasing month-to-month. An increasing pageview count means that more content is being seen across the whole site. Two things could happen to increase the pageviews: more visitors could be coming to the site or visitors could be viewing more pages per visit. Combining the change in pageviews with the change in pages per visit will show which of these scenarios is occurring.

Pages/visit

Dividing total page views by total visits gives the average number of pages that are viewed per visit. Blog-type sites typically have a pages/visit number between 1.5 and 2.

An increasing pages/visit number shows that visitors are clicking on more pages on the site per visit. This is always a beneficial thing but on a content site such as ours, diminishing returns kicks in past 2 pages per visit. Content published, content displayed, and inbound links all contribute to pages/visit.

Bounce rate

The bounce rate is the percentage of people who see one page and leave the site (essentially "bouncing" off of a page). Visitors who bounce have a page/visit number of 1. Bounce rates for blog-type sites are typically around 75%.

A decreasing bounce rate is always a good thing. A decreasing bounce rate means that people found what they wanted and more. Bounce rate is affected by the same things that the pages/visit number is: site design, reader engagement, availability of related content, etc.

Average time on site

This number is the average amount of time that each visit lasts. This figure is tough to report accurately by any analytics programs.

Not a lot of good conclusions can be made from this number by itself. An increasing time, however, could be an indication of reader engagement and attention span. This number can be used in conjunction with bounce rate and pages/visit to get a sense of how involved the readers are and whether this is improving or declining.

% New Visits

This is the percentage of the total visits that came from new visitors. A new visitor is simply someone without our site's cookie present in their browser. As such, this figure has a fairly high margin of error.

Though potentially inaccurate, this is another number whose trends are useful to watch. An increase in % new visits could be an indication of extended online reach or influence while a decrease could mean improved reader engagement. This percentage should show in increase during periods of strong promotion.

Traffic sources (Main > Traffic Sources)

〰️ **24.44%** Direct Traffic		▨ Search Engines 496.00 (58.28%)
〰️ **17.27%** Referring Sites		▨ Direct Traffic 208.00 (24.44%)
〰️ **58.28%** Search Engines		▨ Referring Sites 147.00 (17.27%)

This is the Google triad of traffic sources: direct traffic (people who type our URL in their browser or use a browser-based bookmark), referring sites (a link to our site from another site), and search engines.

There's no right or wrong distribution of traffic sources but a healthy strategy will typically keep each piece close to a third. For a long-tail, content-rich site like ours, the search engine piece should definitely be near one-third. Watching a particular source grow or shrink should correlate to promotions, SEO, or other outreach efforts.

Referring sites (Main > Traffic Sources > Referring Sites)

Visits	Pages/Visit	Avg. Time on Site	% New Visits	Bounce Rate
147	**1.78**	**00:01:10**	**89.12%**	**74.15%**
% of Site Total: 17.27%	Site Avg: 1.53 (16.32%)	Site Avg: 00:01:25 (-17.83%)	Site Avg: 84.96% (4.89%)	Site Avg: 79.55% (-6.79%)

	Dimension: Source ⌄	Visits ↓	Pages/Visit	Avg. Time on Site	% New Visits	Bounce Rate
1.	images.google.com	25	1.32	00:00:19	88.00%	72.00%
2.	twitter.com	22	1.27	00:00:40	86.36%	77.27%
3.	vtv.id.au	10	1.10	00:00:17	90.00%	90.00%
4.	buildbigships.com	5	8.00	00:07:58	40.00%	20.00%
5.	linkedin.com	5	2.00	00:00:16	80.00%	20.00%
6.	filetterpress.com	4	2.00	00:01:13	75.00%	25.00%
7.	forums.vwvortex.com	4	2.75	00:01:31	100.00%	75.00%

This is the list of domains that sent visits to our site. This list also shows visit quality by way of pages/visit, time on site, and bounce rate.

This list can be used to measure the success of site-specific promotions, look for new sites that we might want to partner with, and figure out which sites are sending the best traffic. There might be a community site that we should be interacting with or a social network that is doing well for us.

Keywords (Main > Traffic Sources > Keywords)

This list shows all keywords that were used to find the site via search engines. Like the referring sites, this list also shows traffic quality metrics.

These keywords can be applied directly to on-site SEO efforts. The keywords with the best quality (low bounce rate, high time on site and pages/visit) should be used in post titles, tags, and categories. These can also be used to determine which content gets published and what direction we give bloggers.

Top pages and posts (Main > Content > Top Content/Content by Title)

There are two lists here: by URL and by page title. Some pages share the same title (default) and some are not set which means that the page name list will have some pages combined together. The URL list is an exact list of the pages (just add "http://sitename.com" before each one to get directly to the page).

These lists give an idea of the most popular content on a particular site. These numbers will differ from on-site view counts (likely smaller on Google Analytics) and are a more accurate representation of actual people seeing the content. Tracking the content that gets the most views and has the best traffic quality (fewer exits and bounces) can show content managers the highest performing pages which can help with choosing the right posts on the site.

5 Proven Internet Strategies That Really Grow Your Local Sales

1 VIDEO MARKETING

Would you believe that there are over 26 BILLION videos viewed per month in the United States alone? What's more, YouTube is the #4 search engine on the internet, which means that <u>right now</u> somebody is likely searching for your services online in the form of a video.

Imagine if you had the budget to run infomercials 24 hours a day, 7 days a week... you'd dominate your market! That's the power of video marketing. Let me show you how this is possible on a shoestring (even in a terrible economy!), and be able to engender more trust and respect with your customers than ever before.

#2 LEAD-CAPTURE AND FOLLOW-UP CAMPAIGNS

Did you know that even a GREAT webpage will only convert 5% of it's visitors to a purchase. It's absolutely true, and this means that 19 out of 20 visitors to your website are destined to surf away into the ether... and likely find your competitor's website instead.

However the AVERAGE page that offers consumers <u>free information</u> in exchange for their contact info gets 35-40% conversion.

Imagine being able to instantly increase your return on leads 7-FOLD, and do it with push button automation. This is possible, and I can show you how.

3 LOCAL SEARCH VISIBILITY

Did you know that 65 to 70% of all "buy ready" searches online include a city or local term (like "Milwaukee Plumbing Contractors")?

This means that every search for every term will have the local companies that have figured out how to get listed in all of the local directories.

It goes without saying that your customers can't hire you if they can't find you online. I can make sure that your local business is **found** on Google... for all of the keywords that you need to rank for.

It's important that your neighbors can find you online.

4 SOCIAL MEDIA MARKETING

With over 600,000,000 members, Facebook is a giant that cannot be ignored. Social networks have changed the way people research and make buying decisions.

When leveraged in your favor you'll have the opportunity to build more trust, respect, and credibility than ever before.

Imagine being able to have feedback on how to improve your business, and sell more on a daily basis. Imagine being able to turn every customer into a potential raving fan who will advertise for you. I can make it happen, and you can secure my sevices exclusively in your local market.

5   BLOG MARKETING

Did you know that 77% of all internet users follow one or more blogs? If you're not capitalizing on this growing community, <u>you're missing out on huge business.</u>

Bloggers are passionate about sharing, and if you have one as a client and can turn them into a raving fan, they can propel your business to new heights.

Let me help you create and manage your video blog, all with push-button simplicity so you can leverage this influence-engine giant for your benefit... And increase your bottom line year after year.

About the Author

Author, consultant, and online marketing pro Charles P. Kassotis is an expert at helping small businesses gain a dominant position in their local marketplace.

Charles specializes in helping entrepreneurs and small businesses gain a competitive advantage both online and off. He makes sure that these businesses are able to be "found" on the internet, ensures that they never run out of leads, and helps them to transform these potential clients into lifetime customers (and raving fans!).

If you are serious about improving your own business' bottom line, and would like to schedule a free consultation to see how Charles can set up a comprehensive online marketing campaign for your company, you can contact him by leaving your name, telephone and email address at http://isyourbusinessgoogleable.com/contact or by leaving a voicemail at 1 (561) 935-9362.

A more personal note from me...

Hi,

I'm writing this more personal note, because you know that "About The Author" stuff on the other page, a bit stuffy if you ask me, but my publisher made me put it there...

So, I really hope you enjoyed this book and were able to get some good information out of it.

I've been doing this for a long time both locally here in Boca Raton, FL where I live and Nationally online. I've had the opportunity to work with some truly amazing small business owners and I've had a great time.

In the process I've learned what these folks really need when it comes to creating an online presence, believe me, I've heard the same story a thousand times and I never get tired of it.

Most small business owners are having a hard enough time just fulfilling orders, keeping their shelves stocked and managing employees.

Finding the time to sit in front of a computer and build a website, set up autoresponders, create a facebook page and the list goes on, well, let me just put it this way... Not Gonna Happen.

So I really want to encourage you to find someone that can make this happen for your business, it's vitally important in these times that you have an online presence.

If nothing else, you need to be found on mobile devices like we talked about starting on page 85.

If you're anywhere near Boca Raton, Florida I'd be more than happy to meet up with you and discuss your optons. If you're not, call me anyway, we have quite a few Customers scattered around the country that have really benefitted from getting online.

If you're looking for someone local in your area, we may be able to help you out there as well, I belong to a few groups where us geeks gather and talk shop, and I'd be more than happy to refer you to a colleague closer to you.

Here's all my contact info, I hope to hear from you soon.

Your Friend In Business,

Charles P. Kassotis

(561) 935-9362

http://IsYourBusinessGoogleable.com/contact

Boca Raton, Florida

PS If you know of anyone that might benefit from an online business boost, or that might find the info here-in useful, send me their contact info via the website address above, as well as your info and I'll send them a complimentary copy of this book from you!

PPS When you go to the site above, be sure to visit the homepage and sign up for the free Newsletter. I send out a great article on Mobile Local Marketing just about every week. It's high quality advice on what's working for my clients today. There's also a free report you can download when you sign up. It's easy, just your email address and name is all that's needed.

Free Reports:

I've Put Together A Free Guide To Facebook Marketing For You, You Can Get It Here:

http://IsYourBusinessGoogleable.com/Guide-To-Facebook

I've Put Together A Free Guide To Mobile Marketing For You, You Can Get It Here:

http://IsYourBusinessGoogleable.com/Mobile-Marketing-Guide

I've Also Put Together A Free Guide To Social Media SEO For You, You Can Get It Here:

http://IsYourBusinessGoogleable.com/Social-Media-SEO